Diabetic COOKING

FOR ONE OR TWO

Publications International, Ltd.

Pictured on the front cover *(top to bottom):* Baked Pear Dessert *(page 84)* and Poached Salmon with Dill-Lemon Sauce *(page 46)*.
Pictured on the back cover *(top to bottom):* Couscous Primavera *(page 70)* and Niçoise Salad Wraps *(page 20)*.

ISBN-13: 978-1-4127-5696-9
ISBN-10: 1-4127-5696-0

Manufactured in China.

8 7 6 5 4 3 2 1

Nutritional Analysis: Every effort has been made to check the accuracy of the nutritional information that appears with each recipe. However, because numerous variables account for a wide range of values for certain foods, nutritive analyses in this book should be considered approximate. Different results may be obtained by using different nutrient databases and different brand-name products.

Note: This book is for informational purposes and is not intended to provide medical advice. Neither Publications International, Ltd., nor the authors, editors or publisher takes responsibility for any possible consequences from any treatment, procedure, exercise, dietary modification, action, or applications of medication or preparation by any person reading or following the information in this cookbook. The publication of this book does not constitute the practice of medicine, and this cookbook does not replace your physician, pharmacist or health-care specialist. **Before undertaking any course of treatment or nutritional plan, the authors, editors and publisher advise the reader to check with a physician or other health-care provider.**

Not all recipes in this cookbook are appropriate for all people with diabetes. Health-care providers, registered dietitians and certified diabetes educators can help design specific meal plans tailored to individual needs.

Table of Contents

Cooking for One or Two

Cooking for just yourself or yourself and one other person has many challenges since most recipes make 4 or more servings. That means you may be tempted to eat more than one serving. Or, you must deal with leftovers tomorrow. Sometimes it just seems easier to buy a frozen meal, carry-out food or even fast food. For people with diabetes every meal is important and the challenge to make it a healthy one is always present. *Diabetic Cooking for One or Two* is the perfect solution to these problems.

About the Recipes

The recipes in *Diabetic Cooking for One or Two* were specifically developed for people with diabetes. All are based on the principals of sound nutrition as outlined by the Dietary Guidelines for Americans developed by the United States Department of Health and Human Services.

Although the recipes are not intended as a medically therapeutic program, nor as a substitute for medically approved meal plans for individuals with diabetes, they contain controlled amounts of calories, fat, cholesterol, sodium and carbohydrate that will fit easily into an individualized meal plan designed by your physician, certified diabetes educator or registered dietitian, and you.

The goal of this publication is to provide a variety of recipe choices for people with diabetes. Since diabetic meal plans can vary a great deal from one individual to another, not all recipes may be suitable for every person with diabetes. Therefore, each individual must choose wisely from among the recipes in this book based on information provided by professionals and their past experience.

Cooking Equipment

Most of the recipes in this publication require skillets and saucepans that you use every day. Some of the recipes require small casseroles or baking dishes (1½ cups to 1½ quarts). If you don't have these, look for inexpensive 4-cup and 6-cup ovenproof, microwavable storage containers. Large custard cups, individual soufflé dishes, 7×5-inch baking dishes and small gratin dishes are also excellent choices. Unless they are marked as microwave-safe, use these casseroles only in a conventional oven. A small scale can be a useful, but not necessary, tool for measuring fruits, vegetables, meat and small amounts of pasta.

A Few Words about Sugar

In 1994, the American Diabetes Association lifted the absolute ban on sugar from the recommended dietary guidelines for people with diabetes. Under updated guidelines, you can, for example, exchange 1 tablespoon of sugar for a slice of bread because each is considered a starch exchange. The new guidelines for sugar intake are based on scientific studies that show that carbohydrate in the form of sugars do not raise blood glucose levels any more rapidly than other types of carbohydrate-containing food. What is more important is the total amount of carbohydrate eaten, not the source.

However, keep in mind that sweets and other foods high in sugar are usually high in calories and fat and contain few, if any, other nutrients, so the choice between an apple and a doughnut is still an easy one to make. Nobody, diabetic or not, should be eating foods filled with lots of sugar. But, when calculated into the nutritional analysis, a small amount of sugar can enhance a recipe and will not be harmful.

If you have any questions or concerns about incorporating sugar into your daily meal plans, consult your physician and certified diabetes educator or registered dietitian for more information.

Nutritional Analysis

The nutritional analysis that appears with each recipe was calculated by an independent nutritional consulting firm. Every effort has been made to check the accuracy of these numbers. However, because numerous variables account for a wide range of values in certain foods, all analyses that appear in this publication should be considered approximate.

• The analysis of each recipe includes all the ingredients that are listed in that recipe, except those labeled as "optional." Nutritional analysis is provided for the primary recipe only, not the recipe variations.

• If a range of amounts is offered for an ingredient (1 to 1¼ cups), the first amount given was used to calculate the nutritional information.

• If an ingredient is presented with an option ("1 cup hot cooked rice or noodles" for example), the first item listed was used to calculate the nutritional information.

• Foods shown in photographs on the same serving plate or offered as "serving suggestions" at the end of the recipe are not included in the recipe analysis unless they are listed in the ingredient list.

• In recipes calling for cooked rice or pasta or calling for rice or pasta to be cooked according to package directions, the analysis was based on preparation without salt and fat.

Soups & Stews

French Onion Soup for Deux

  2 teaspoons olive oil
¾ pound yellow onions, halved lengthwise and cut into thin slices
  1 clove garlic, thinly sliced
¼ teaspoon black pepper
⅛ teaspoon salt
  1 cup water
  1 cup fat-free reduced-sodium chicken broth
  1 tablespoon balsamic vinegar
  1 bay leaf
½ teaspoon dried thyme
  2 thick slices crusty whole wheat bread, toasted
¼ cup (1 ounce) shredded reduced-fat Muenster or Monterey Jack cheese

1. Heat oil in large saucepan over medium heat. Add onions and garlic. Cook and stir 20 minutes or until onions are soft and golden brown. If onions start to stick or burn, reduce heat slightly and add water one tablespoon at a time. Sprinkle onions with pepper and salt.

2. Reduce heat to low; add 1 cup water, broth, vinegar, bay leaf and thyme. Simmer until heated through. Discard bay leaf.

3. Preheat broiler. Place 2 ovenproof bowls on baking sheet. Ladle soup into bowls; top each with toasted bread. Sprinkle with cheese. Broil 1 minute or until cheese melts and is bubbly and browned. *Makes 2 servings*

Nutrients per Serving: 1½ cups soup with 1 slice bread and 2 tablespoons cheese

Calories: 306, Calories from Fat: 35 %, Total Fat: 12 g, Saturated Fat: 4 g, Cholesterol: 28 mg, Sodium: 549 mg, Carbohydrate: 37 g, Fiber: 6 g, Protein: 14 g

Dietary Exchanges: 1 Vegetable, 2 Starch, 1 Meat, 2 Fat

Chickpea and Orange Squash Stew

    1 teaspoon canola oil
    ¾ cup chopped onion
    ½ to 1 jalapeño pepper,* seeded and minced
    ½ inch piece fresh ginger, peeled and minced
    1 clove garlic, minced
    2 teaspoons ground cumin
    ½ teaspoon ground coriander
    1 cup cubed peeled orange squash, sweet potato or pumpkin
    1 cup no-salt-added canned chickpeas, rinsed and drained
    ½ cup water
    ½ tablespoon reduced-sodium soy sauce
    1 cup reduced-fat coconut milk**
      Juice of 1 lime
    ¼ cup chopped fresh cilantro leaves
      Baby spinach (optional)

*Jalapeño peppers can sting and irritate the skin, so wear rubber gloves when handling peppers and do not touch your eyes.

**Leftover coconut milk can be frozen for later use.

1. Heat oil in medium saucepan over medium-low heat. Add onion, pepper, ginger and garlic; cook and stir 2 to 3 minutes or until onion is translucent but does not brown. Add cumin and coriander; cook and stir 1 minute.

2. Add squash, beans, water and soy sauce. Bring to a boil. Reduce heat and simmer 15 minutes or until squash is tender and water is nearly evaporated. Add coconut milk and heat through. Add lime juice and cilantro; stir to blend. Garnish with spinach.

Makes 2 servings

Nutrients per Serving: 1½ cups vegetables and beans with ½ cup sauce

Calories: 300, Calories from Fat: 33 %, Total Fat: 11 g, Saturated Fat: 4 g, Cholesterol: 0 mg, Sodium: 204 mg, Carbohydrate: 42 g, Fiber: 10 g, Protein: 10 g

Dietary Exchanges: 3 Starch, 2 Fat

Turkey Albondigas Soup

¼ cup uncooked brown rice

Meatballs
  ½ pound ground lean turkey
  1 tablespoon minced onion
  1 teaspoon chopped cilantro
  1 teaspoon fat-free (skim) milk
  ½ teaspoon hot pepper sauce
  ⅛ teaspoon dried oregano
  ⅛ teaspoon black pepper

Broth
  1 teaspoon olive oil
  2 tablespoons chopped onion
  1 clove garlic, minced
  2½ cups fat-free reduced-sodium chicken broth
  2 teaspoons hot pepper sauce
  1 teaspoon tomato paste
  ⅛ teaspoon black pepper
  3 small carrots, cut into rounds (about 1 cup)
  ½ medium zucchini, quartered and sliced
  ½ yellow crookneck squash, quartered and sliced

Garnish (optional)
    Lime wedges
    Cilantro leaves

1. Prepare rice according to package directions, omitting salt and fat.

2. Meanwhile, combine meatball ingredients in large bowl; mix until blended. Shape into 1-inch meatballs; set aside.

3. Heat oil in medium saucepan over medium heat. Add onion and garlic; cook and stir 1 minute. Add broth, hot pepper sauce, tomato paste and pepper. Bring to a boil over high heat; reduce heat to a simmer.

4. Drop meatballs and carrots into broth; simmer 15 minutes. Add zucchini, squash and cooked rice. Simmer 5 to 10 minutes or until vegetables are just tender.

5. Garnish with lime wedges and cilantro, if desired. Serve immediately.

Makes 2 servings

continued on page 14

Turkey Albondigas Soup, continued

Nutrients per Serving: ½ of total recipe

Calories: 342, Calories from Fat: 29 %, Total Fat: 11 g, Saturated Fat: 3 g, Cholesterol: 70 mg, Sodium: 404 mg, Carbohydrate: 32 g, Fiber: 5 g, Protein: 30 g

Dietary Exchanges: 2 Starch, 3 Meat, ½ Fat

Chunky Chicken Stew

1 teaspoon olive oil
1 small onion, chopped
1 cup thinly sliced carrots
1 cup fat-free reduced-sodium chicken broth
1 can (about 14 ounces) no-salt-added diced tomatoes
1 cup diced cooked chicken breast
3 cups sliced kale or baby spinach

1. Heat oil in large saucepan over medium-high heat. Add onion; cook and stir 5 minutes or until golden brown. Stir in carrots and broth; bring to a boil. Reduce heat; simmer, uncovered, 5 minutes.

2. Add tomatoes; simmer 5 minutes or until carrots are tender. Add chicken; cook and stir until heated through. Add kale; cook and stir 1 minute.   *Makes 2 servings*

Nutrients per Serving: ½ of total recipe

Calories: 287, Calories from Fat: 18 %, Total Fat: 6 g, Saturated Fat: 1 g, Cholesterol: 66 mg, Sodium: 337 mg, Carbohydrate: 31 g, Fiber: 8 g, Protein: 30 g

Dietary Exchanges: 6 Vegetable, 3 Meat

French Peasant Soup

    1 slice lean bacon, chopped
    ½ cup diced carrots
    ½ cup diced celery
    ¼ cup minced onion
    1 clove garlic, minced
    2 tablespoons white wine or water
 1½ cups fat-free reduced-sodium vegetable broth
    1 bay leaf
    1 sprig fresh thyme *or* 1 teaspoon dried thyme
    1 sprig fresh parsley *or* 1 teaspoon dried parsley
    ½ cup chopped green beans (½-inch pieces)
    2 tablespoons uncooked small pasta or elbow macaroni
    ½ cup no-salt-added canned cannellini beans, rinsed and drained
    ½ cup diced zucchini
    ¼ cup chopped leek
    2 teaspoons prepared pesto sauce
    2 teaspoons grated Parmesan cheese

1. Cook bacon in medium saucepan over medium heat 3 minutes or until partially cooked; drain fat. Add carrots, celery, onion and garlic; cook and stir 5 minutes or until carrots are crisp-tender. Stir in wine; simmer until most of wine has evaporated. Add broth, bay leaf, thyme and parsley; simmer 10 minutes.

2. Add green beans; simmer 5 minutes. Add pasta; cook 5 to 7 minutes or until almost tender.

3. Add cannellini beans, zucchini and leek; cook 3 to 5 minutes or until vegetables are tender.

4. Remove and discard bay leaf. Ladle soup into 2 bowls. Stir 1 teaspoon pesto into each bowl and sprinkle with 1 teaspoon cheese.   *Makes 2 servings*

Nutrients per Serving: ½ of total recipe

Calories: 192, Calories from Fat: 16 %, Total Fat: 3 g, Saturated Fat: 1 g, Cholesterol: 6 mg, Sodium: 499 mg, Carbohydrate: 30 g, Fiber: 7 g, Protein: 9 g

Dietary Exchanges: 1½ Starch, 1 Fat

Vietnamese Beef and Noodle Soup

    4 cups water
    2 ounces whole wheat angel hair pasta, broken in half
2¼ cups fat-free reduced-sodium beef broth
    1 shallot, sliced
    1 star anise (optional)
    ½ teaspoon minced fresh ginger
    1 teaspoon fish sauce or reduced-sodium soy sauce
    1 teaspoon reduced-sodium soy sauce
    ½ teaspoon hot pepper sauce
    6 ounces boneless beef sirloin, sliced ⅛ inch thick
    ⅛ teaspoon salt
    ⅛ teaspoon black pepper
    1 cup bean sprouts
    2 green onions, thinly sliced
    1 small fresh red chile, thinly sliced (optional)
    2 lime wedges (optional)
    2 tablespoons cilantro leaves (optional)

1. Bring water to a boil in medium saucepan. Cook pasta about 3 to 4 minutes or until tender. Drain; set aside.

2. Bring broth, shallot, star anise, if desired, and ginger to a boil in another medium saucepan. Reduce heat and simmer 10 minutes. Strain. Stir in fish sauce, soy sauce and hot pepper sauce.

3. Season beef with salt and pepper. Add beef and bean sprouts to broth mixture. Cook 2 minutes or until beef is no longer pink. Add pasta and green onions; stir well.

4. Ladle soup into 2 bowls. Garnish with chile, lime wedges and cilantro.

Makes 2 servings

Nutrients per Serving: ½ of total recipe

Calories: 258, Calories from Fat: 21 %, Total Fat: 6 g, Saturated Fat: 2 g, Cholesterol: 40 mg, Sodium: 515 mg, Carbohydrate: 27 g, Fiber: 5 g, Protein: 23 g

Dietary Exchanges: 2 Starch, 2 Meat

Sandwiches & Salads

Niçoise Salad Wraps

½ cup chopped green beans

2 baby red potatoes, each cut into 8 wedges

2 tablespoons reduced-fat vinaigrette, divided

1 egg

2 cups watercress leaves

4 ounces albacore tuna packed in water, drained and flaked (about ½ cup)

8 niçoise olives, pitted and halved

3 cherry tomatoes, quartered

2 (10-inch) whole wheat tortillas

1. Bring 8 cups water to a boil in large saucepan. Add green beans and potatoes. Reduce heat to low; simmer 6 minutes or until tender. Remove vegetables with slotted spoon; immerse in ice water to stop cooking. Drain on paper towels. Transfer to medium bowl; toss with 1 tablespoon vinaigrette.

2. Bring water back to a boil. Add whole egg; reduce heat and simmer 12 minutes. Cool in ice water. Peel and cut into 4 wedges.

3. Add watercress, tuna, olives, tomatoes and remaining 1 tablespoon vinaigrette to vegetables; toss gently.

4. Heat tortillas in nonstick skillet over medium-high heat, turning once. Place on 2 plates.

5. Divide salad between tortillas; top with egg wedges. Roll up tortillas to enclose filling. Cut each roll in half before serving. *Makes 2 servings*

Nutrients per Serving: 1 wrap

Calories: 306, Calories from Fat: 27 %, Total Fat: 11 g, Saturated Fat: 1 g, Cholesterol: 120 mg, Sodium: 833 mg, Carbohydrate: 43 g, Fiber: 18 g, Protein: 24 g

Dietary Exchanges: 2 Vegetable, 2 Starch, 2 Meat

Greek-Style Chicken and Bread Salad

    2 slices stale whole wheat bread
    1 clove garlic, halved
    1 cup diced cooked chicken breast
    1 cup halved cherry or grape tomatoes
    1 small cucumber, peeled and diced
    ¼ cup thinly sliced green onions (green parts only) or ¼ cup thinly
        sliced red onion
  2½ tablespoons reduced-sodium chicken broth
    4 teaspoons lemon juice
    ½ teaspoon olive oil
    ¼ teaspoon dried oregano
    ⅛ teaspoon black pepper
    ⅛ teaspoon salt (optional)

1. Toast or grill bread until lightly browned and crisp. Rub 1 side of each bread slice with garlic. Tear into bite-size pieces. Combine bread, chicken, tomatoes, cucumber and green onions in large salad bowl. Toss gently to combine.

2. Stir together broth, lemon juice, oil, oregano and pepper in small bowl. Pour over salad. Toss gently to combine. Season with salt, if desired.   *Makes 2 servings*

Variation: Use only 1 slice of bread instead of 2 for a reduction of 100 calories, 2g fat, 4g protein, 20g carbohydrate, 3g fiber and 180mg sodium.

Nutrients per Serving: 1½ cups salad

Calories: 304, Calories from Fat: 24 %, Total Fat: 8 g, Saturated Fat: 1 g, Cholesterol: 54 mg, Sodium: 222 mg, Carbohydrate: 33 g, Fiber: 5 g, Protein: 26 g

Dietary Exchanges: 2 Starch, 3 Meat

Cucumber Cheese Melts

1 ounce fat-free cream cheese, softened
1 tablespoon crumbled blue cheese
4 slices multi-grain bread
2 tablespoons sugar-free apricot fruit spread
8 cucumber slices
1 ounce thinly sliced reduced-sodium ham
2 slices (1½ ounces) fat-free Swiss cheese
   Butter-flavored cooking spray

1. Mix cream cheese and blue cheese in small bowl. Spread on 2 bread slices. Spread fruit spread over cheeses on each slice. Top each with 4 cucumber slices, ham, Swiss cheese and remaining bread slice.

2. Lightly spray medium skillet with cooking spray. Heat over medium heat. Cook sandwiches 4 minutes or until bottoms are browned. Spray tops of sandwiches with cooking spray; turn. Cook 4 minutes or until browned on other side.

3. Cut sandwiches into 4 slices before serving, if desired.   *Makes 2 servings*

Nutrients per Serving: 1 sandwich (4 slices)

Calories: 246, Calories from Fat: 15 %, Total Fat: 5 g, Saturated Fat: 1 g, Cholesterol: 12 mg, Sodium: 743 mg, Carbohydrate: 40 g, Fiber: 8 g, Protein: 17 g

Dietary Exchanges: ½ Fruit, 2 Starch, 2 Meat

Turkey Club Salad

8 large romaine lettuce leaves
8 thin slices reduced-fat reduced-sodium deli-style turkey breast (about
   4 ounces)
2 medium tomatoes, thinly sliced
2 tablespoons soy-based imitation bacon bits or real bacon bits
¼ cup fat-free ranch salad dressing
   Black pepper (optional)

Layer lettuce, turkey, tomatoes and bacon bits on 2 plates. Drizzle with dressing. Season
with pepper, if desired.   *Makes 2 servings*

Nutrients per Serving: ½ of total recipe

Calories: 170, Calories from Fat: 15 %, Total Fat: 3 g, Saturated Fat: <1 g, Cholesterol: 23 mg,
Sodium: 521 mg, Carbohydrate: 18 g, Fiber: 4 g, Protein: 17 g

Dietary Exchanges: 3 Vegetable, 2 Meat

Mediterranean Chicken Salad

2 cups spring salad greens or mesclun
½ cup diced cooked chicken breast
1 plum tomato, sliced
¼ cup fat-free croutons
2 tablespoons chopped fresh basil
2 tablespoons reduced-fat reduced-sodium Italian salad dressing
   Black pepper (optional)

1. Combine greens, chicken, tomato, croutons, basil and dressing in large bowl;
toss well.

2. Transfer mixture to plate. Season with pepper, if desired.   *Makes 1 serving*

Nutrients per Serving: 1 salad

Calories: 187, Calories from Fat: 17 %, Total Fat: 3 g, Saturated Fat: <1 g, Cholesterol: 56 mg,
Sodium: 587 mg, Carbohydrate: 14 g, Fiber: 3 g, Protein: 23 g

Dietary Exchanges: 1 Vegetable, ½ Starch, 2 Meat

Honey-Mustard Chicken Salad

1 can (about 4 ounces) low-sodium white chicken, rinsed and drained
½ cup quartered seedless red grapes
¼ cup chopped water chestnuts
2 tablespoons fat-free reduced-sodium honey-mustard salad dressing
¼ teaspoon grated lemon peel
1 cup fresh baby spinach
1 teaspoon pine nuts
⅛ teaspoon black pepper

1. Toss chicken, grapes, water chestnuts, dressing and lemon peel together in small bowl until well coated. Let stand 5 minutes for dressing to absorb.

2. Toast pine nuts in small nonstick skillet over medium-low heat 2 minutes, shaking pan constantly. Remove from heat.

3. Arrange spinach on plate; top with chicken mixture. Sprinkle pine nuts on top; season with pepper.   *Makes 1 serving*

Nutrients per Serving: 1 salad

Calories: 213, Calories from Fat: 14 %, Total Fat: 4 g, Saturated Fat: <1 g, Cholesterol: 27 mg, Sodium: 603 mg, Carbohydrate: 33 g, Fiber: 2 g, Protein: 17 g

Dietary Exchanges: 1 Fruit, 1 Starch, 2 Meat

Hoisin-Orange Chicken Wraps

2 tablespoons hoisin sauce
¼ teaspoon grated orange peel
2 tablespoons orange juice
4 whole Boston lettuce leaves
1 cup shredded coleslaw mix
1 cup diced cooked chicken breast (about 4 ounces)
   Black pepper (optional)

1. Combine hoisin sauce, orange peel and juice in small bowl.

2. Arrange lettuce leaves on large serving platter. Place ¼ cup coleslaw mix, ¼ cup chicken and 1 tablespoon hoisin mixture on each leaf. Sprinkle with pepper, if desired. Fold lettuce over to create wraps.   *Makes 2 servings*

Nutrients per Serving: 2 wraps

Calories: 168, Calories from Fat: 15 %, Total Fat: 3 g, Saturated Fat: <1 g, Cholesterol: 54 mg, Sodium: 314 mg, Carbohydrate: 13 g, Fiber: 2 g, Protein: 22 g

Dietary Exchanges: 1 Vegetable, 3 Meat

Tip

Cabbage, found in coleslaw mix, is a nutrient dense vegetable. It packs important antioxidants and vitamin C and will also give you a fiber boost to help keep you full.

Finger-Lickin' Chicken Salad

½ cup diced cooked chicken breast
½ stalk celery, cut into 1-inch pieces
¼ cup drained mandarin orange segments
¼ cup red seedless grapes
2 tablespoons lemon sugar-free fat-free yogurt
1 tablespoon reduced-fat mayonnaise
¼ teaspoon reduced-sodium soy sauce
⅛ teaspoon pumpkin pie spice or cinnamon

1. Toss chicken, celery, oranges and grapes together in small bowl.

2. Combine yogurt, mayonnaise, soy sauce and pumpkin pie spice in another small bowl or cup.

3. Serve dipping sauce with chicken mixture.   *Makes 1 serving*

Variation: Thread the chicken onto wooden skewers alternately with celery, oranges and grapes.

Note: This salad is a quick and nutritious meal on the go. Pack the chicken mixture and dipping sauce in covered plastic containers, then pack them into an insulated bag with an ice pack.

Nutrients per Serving: 1 salad

Calories: 207, Calories from Fat: 25 %, Total Fat: 6 g, Saturated Fat: 1 g, Cholesterol: 64 mg, Sodium: 212 mg, Carbohydrate: 15 g, Fiber: 1 g, Protein: 24 g

Dietary Exchanges: 1 Fruit, 3 Meat

Lettuce Wrap Enchiladas

Nonstick cooking spray
1 *each* red and green bell peppers, seeded and sliced into ¼-inch strips
2 tablespoons water
½ tablespoon chili powder
1 cup shredded or cubed cooked chicken breast or thigh
½ cup fresh cilantro, chopped
8 romaine lettuce leaves
½ cup fat-free reduced-sodium refried beans, warmed
½ cup salsa
½ cup (2 ounces) shredded reduced-fat Cheddar cheese
¼ cup fat-free sour cream

1. Lightly spray large skillet with cooking spray. Heat over medium-high heat. Add pepper strips, water and chili powder. Cook 4 to 5 minutes or until water evaporates, stirring occasionally. Reduce heat to low. Add chicken; heat until warm. Stir in cilantro. Cover; remove from heat.

2. Make 4 enchilada wrappers by lining 1 large romaine leaf with 1 small leaf per wrap.

3. Spread each wrapper with one fourth of beans and one fourth of chicken mixture. Top each with 2 tablespoons salsa and 2 tablespoons cheese. Serve with sour cream.

Makes 2 servings

Nutrients per Serving: 2 enchiladas

Calories: 290, Calories from Fat: 9 %, Total Fat: 9 g, Saturated Fat: 4 g, Cholesterol: 79 mg, Sodium: 651 mg, Carbohydrate: 21 g, Fiber: 6 g, Protein: 33 g

Dietary Exchanges: 1 Starch, 1 Meat, 1 Fat

Antipasto Italian Roll-Ups

1 tablespoon fat-free sour cream
1 tablespoon sun-dried tomato spread
2 (6-inch) whole wheat tortillas
½ cup fresh basil leaves
⅓ cup chopped roasted red bell pepper
2 ounces part-skim mozzarella cheese, thinly sliced
1 ounce thinly sliced reduced-fat salami

Combine sour cream and sun-dried tomato spread in small bowl. Spread 1 tablespoon tomato mixture down center of each tortilla. Top each with half of basil, bell pepper, mozzarella cheese and salami. Roll up. *Makes 2 servings*

Nutrients per Serving: 1 roll-up

Calories: 251, Calories from Fat: 39 %, Total Fat: 11 g, Saturated Fat: 4 g, Cholesterol: 36 mg, Sodium: 715 mg, Carbohydrate: 24 g, Fiber: 3 g, Protein: 14 g

Dietary Exchanges: 1 Vegetable, 1 Starch, 2 Meat, 1 Fat

Waldorf Chicken Salad

2 tablespoons fat-free mayonnaise
2 tablespoons fat-free sour cream
1 cup chopped unpeeled apples
½ cup chopped celery
⅓ cup chopped cooked chicken breast
2 teaspoons chopped walnuts
4 romaine lettuce leaves

1. Mix mayonnaise and sour cream in small bowl.

2. Toss apples, celery and chicken in medium bowl. Add dressing; toss to combine. Sprinkle walnuts on top; serve over lettuce leaves. *Makes 2 servings*

Nutrients per Serving: 1 cup salad

Calories: 112, Calories from Fat: 20 %, Total Fat: 3 g, Saturated Fat: <1 g, Cholesterol: 20 mg, Sodium: 178 mg, Carbohydrate: 14 g, Fiber: 2 g, Protein: 9 g

Dietary Exchanges: 1 Fruit, 1 Meat

Double Mango Shrimp Salad

    3 tablespoons picante sauce or salsa
    1 tablespoon mango or peach chutney
    1 tablespoon Dijon mustard
    1 tablespoon lime juice
    4 cups torn Boston or red leaf lettuce
    6 ounces medium cooked shrimp, peeled and deveined
    ½ cup diced ripe avocado
    ½ cup diced ripe mango or papaya
    ⅓ cup red or yellow bell pepper strips
    2 tablespoons chopped fresh cilantro (optional)

1. Combine picante sauce, chutney, mustard and lime juice in small bowl; mix well.

2. Combine lettuce, shrimp, avocado, mango, bell pepper and cilantro, if desired, in medium bowl. Add chutney mixture; toss well. Serve immediately.

Makes 2 servings

Nutrients per Serving: 2¼ cups salad

Calories: 221, Calories from Fat: 28 %, Total Fat: 7 g, Saturated Fat: 1 g, Cholesterol: 166 mg, Sodium: 583 mg, Carbohydrate: 19 g, Fiber: 4 g, Protein: 21 g

Dietary Exchanges: 1 Fruit, 3 Meat

Tip

There are hundreds of varieties of mangoes. Select fruit that feels firm but yields to slight pressure.

Crab Louis Stuffed Tomatoes

2 large ripe tomatoes
3 tablespoons reduced-fat sour cream
3 tablespoons reduced-sodium ketchup or chili sauce
2 tablespoons chopped chives or green onion tops
1 teaspoon prepared horseradish
½ pound imitation crabmeat, shredded*
2 large Boston or red leaf lettuce leaves

*8 ounces fresh or pasteurized lump crabmeat or 2 (6-ounce) cans blue crabmeat, drained and flaked, may be substituted.

1. Cut tomatoes in half crosswise. Push out and discard seeds. Cut out pulp from each tomato half, leaving shells intact. Chop pulp.

2. Stir tomato pulp, sour cream, ketchup, chives and horseradish in medium bowl. Stir in crabmeat; spoon mixture into tomato shells. Serve on 2 lettuce-lined plates.

Makes 2 servings

Nutrients per Serving: 2 tomato halves with ½ of crabmeat mixture

Calories: 218, Calories from Fat: 18 %, Total Fat: 5 g, Saturated Fat: 2 g, Cholesterol: 31 mg, Sodium: 994 mg, Carbohydrate: 28 g, Fiber: 4 g, Protein: 28 g

Dietary Exchanges: 2 Vegetable, 1 Starch, 2 Meat

Tip

Read the labels on various brands of imitation crabmeat to find the one with the lowest sodium content.

Shortcut Calzones

½ cup cooked ground sirloin, broken up
⅔ cup cherry tomatoes, halved and seeded
⅓ cup frozen chopped spinach, thawed and squeezed dry
¼ cup chopped yellow onion
1 tablespoon minced green olives
½ teaspoon minced garlic
4 ready-to-use frozen dinner roll dough balls, thawed (about 1.3 ounces per roll)
1 tablespoon flour for rolling out dough
1 tablespoon tomato paste
2 tablespoons shredded reduced-fat mozzarella cheese
½ cup reduced-fat reduced-sodium marinara sauce

1. Preheat oven to 425°F. Spray baking sheet with nonstick cooking spray.

2. Mix together ground beef, tomatoes, spinach, onion, olives and garlic in large bowl; set aside.

3. Roll out each dough ball on floured surface until thin. Lay 2 dough pieces on baking sheet. Spread each piece with half of tomato paste. Top each with half of beef mixture and 1 tablespoon cheese. Cover with remaining 2 dough pieces. Pinch dough edges together to seal.

4. Bake 15 minutes or until golden and heated through. Cut each calzone in half and serve immediately. Serve with marinara sauce for dipping.   *Makes 2 servings*

Nutrients per Serving: 1 calzone

Calories: 351, Calories from Fat: 22 %, Total Fat: 9 g, Saturated Fat: 2 g, Cholesterol: 20 mg, Sodium: 912 mg, Carbohydrate: 51 g, Fiber: 7 g, Protein: 17 g

Dietary Exchanges: 1 Vegetable, 3 Starch, 1 Meat, 1 Fat

Main Dishes

Roasted Almond Tilapia

2 tilapia or Boston scrod fillets (6 ounces each)
¼ teaspoon salt
1 tablespoon prepared mustard
¼ cup whole wheat bread crumbs
2 tablespoons chopped almonds
   Paprika (optional)
   Lemon wedges

1. Preheat oven to 450°F. Place fish on small baking sheet; season with salt. Spread mustard over fish. Combine bread crumbs and almonds in small bowl; sprinkle over fish. Press lightly to adhere. Sprinkle with paprika, if desired.

2. Bake 8 to 10 minutes or until fish begins to flake when tested with fork. Serve with lemon wedges, if desired. *Makes 2 servings*

Nutrients per Serving: 1 fillet

Calories: 268, Calories from Fat: 32 %, Total Fat: 10 g, Saturated Fat: <1 g, Cholesterol: 0 mg, Sodium: 587 mg, Carbohydrate: 14 g, Fiber: 2 g, Protein: 32 g

Dietary Exchanges: 1 Starch, 2 Fat

Poached Salmon with Dill-Lemon Sauce

3 cups water
1 cup white wine
1 shallot, sliced into rings
   Peel of 1 lemon
2 sprigs fresh parsley
1 sprig fresh dill plus ½ teaspoon chopped fresh dill, divided
3 black peppercorns
1 salmon fillet (6 ounces), about 1 inch thick
¾ teaspoon lemon juice
½ teaspoon canola oil
1 tablespoon low-fat mayonnaise
1 tablespoon milk
   Additional fresh dill sprig (optional)

1. Combine water, wine, shallot, lemon peel, parsley, dill sprig and peppercorns in medium saucepan. Bring to a simmer. (Do not boil.) Simmer gently 15 minutes.

2. Reduce heat to just below simmering. Place salmon in liquid; cook 4 to 5 minutes or until fish begins to flake when tested with fork.

3. Meanwhile, combine lemon juice and canola oil in small bowl; stir well. Add mayonnaise; beat well. Mixture may look separated but will come together after mixing. Stir in milk, 1 teaspoon at a time, beating well between each addition. Mix in chopped dill just before serving.

4. Transfer salmon to serving plate. Spoon dill-lemon sauce on top; garnish with dill sprig. *Makes 1 serving*

Serving Suggestion: Serve salmon with steamed asparagus and couscous.

Nutrients per Serving: Total recipe

Calories: 387, Calories from Fat: 55 %, Total Fat: 23 g, Saturated Fat: 6 g, Cholesterol: 89 mg, Sodium: 169 mg, Carbohydrate: 4 g, Fiber: 0 g, Protein: 35 g

Dietary Exchanges: 5 Meat, 2½ Fat

Szechuan Pork Stir-Fry over Spinach

  2 teaspoons dark sesame oil, divided
¾ cup matchstick-size carrot strips
½ pound lean pork tenderloin, cut into thin strips
  3 cloves garlic, minced
  2 teaspoons minced fresh ginger
¼ to ½ teaspoon red pepper flakes
  1 tablespoon reduced-sodium soy sauce
  1 tablespoon mirin* or dry sherry
  2 teaspoons cornstarch
  8 ounces baby spinach
  2 teaspoons sesame seeds, toasted**

Mirin, a sweet wine made from rice, is an essential flavoring in Japanese cuisine. It is available in Asian markets and the Asian or gourmet section of some supermarkets.

**To toast sesame seeds, spread in small skillet. Shake skillet over medium-low heat about 3 minutes or until seeds begin to pop and turn golden. Remove from heat.*

1. Heat 1 teaspoon oil in large nonstick skillet over medium-high heat. Add carrot strips; cook and stir 3 minutes. Add pork, garlic, ginger and red pepper flakes to taste. Stir-fry 3 minutes or until pork is no longer pink.

2. Stir soy sauce, mirin and cornstarch in small bowl until well blended; add to pork mixture. Stir-fry about 1 minute or until sauce thickens.

3. Heat remaining 1 teaspoon oil in medium saucepan over medium-high heat. Add spinach. Cover and cook until spinach is barely wilted, about 1 minute. Transfer spinach to 2 serving plates. Spoon pork mixture over spinach. Sprinkle with sesame seeds.

Makes 2 servings

Nutrients per Serving: 2 cups stir-fry

Calories: 270, Calories from Fat: 32 %, Total Fat: 10 g, Saturated Fat: 2 g, Cholesterol: 73 mg, Sodium: 971 mg, Carbohydrate: 13 g, Fiber: 3 g, Protein: 31 g

Dietary Exchanges: 2 Vegetable, 4 Meat

Deviled Crab Bake

1 can (6½ ounces) crabmeat, drained
2 teaspoons canola oil
½ cup diced onion
½ cup diced green pepper
¼ cup diced celery
1 cup fresh bread crumbs
¼ cup milk
1 tablespoon lemon juice
1 teaspoon dried dill
   Pinch ground red pepper or seafood seasoning mix to taste
   Black pepper

1. Preheat oven to 375°F. Pick out and discard any shell or cartilage from crabmeat.

2. Heat oil in ovenproof skillet over medium heat. Add onion, green pepper and celery; cook and stir 2 to 3 minutes or until onion is translucent and vegetables are crisp-tender. Remove from heat and set aside.

3. Place bread crumbs in large bowl. Slowly pour milk over crumbs to moisten, stirring lightly. Let stand 5 minutes.

4. Add crabmeat, vegetables, lemon juice, dill, red pepper and black pepper to moistened bread crumbs. Stir lightly to blend. Spoon mixture back into skillet. Bake about 15 minutes or until lightly browned. *Makes 2 servings*

Serving Suggestion: Garnish with fresh dill sprigs and lemon wedges.

Nutrients per Serving: 1½ cups

Calories: 210, Calories from Fat: 29 %, Total Fat: 7 g, Saturated Fat: 1 g, Cholesterol: 86 mg, Sodium: 830 mg, Carbohydrate: 20 g, Fiber: 2 g, Protein: 17 g

Dietary Exchanges: 1 Starch, 2 Meat

Cajun Chicken Drums

    4 chicken drumsticks, skin removed
    ½ to ¾ teaspoon Cajun seasoning
    ½ teaspoon grated lemon peel
    2 tablespoons lemon juice
    ½ teaspoon hot pepper sauce
    ⅛ teaspoon salt
    2 tablespoons chopped fresh parsley (optional)

1. Preheat oven to 400°F. Coat shallow baking dish with nonstick cooking spray. Arrange chicken in dish; sprinkle evenly with Cajun seasoning. Cover dish with foil; bake 25 minutes, turning drumsticks once.

2. Remove foil; bake 15 to 20 minutes longer or until cooked through and juices run clear (165°F). Combine lemon peel, lemon juice, hot pepper sauce and salt in small bowl; pour over chicken. Sprinkle with parsley, if desired. Serve immediately.

Makes 2 servings

Nutrients per Serving: 2 drumsticks

Calories: 173, Calories from Fat: 25 %, Total Fat: 5 g, Saturated Fat: 1 g, Cholesterol: 108 mg, Sodium: 254 mg, Carbohydrate: 2 g, Fiber: <1 g, Protein: 29 g

Dietary Exchanges: 1 Fat, 3 Meat

Tip

Boneless skinless chicken breasts would also work well in this recipe. Just check that they are no longer pink in the center at the end of the cooking time.

Breakfast Pizza

2 cups refrigerated or frozen shredded hash brown potatoes, thawed
½ cup finely chopped onion
　Nonstick cooking spray
¼ cup tomato paste
2 tablespoons water
½ teaspoon dried oregano
½ cup cholesterol-free egg substitute
½ cup (2 ounces) shredded mozzarella cheese
2 tablespoons imitation bacon bits

1. Combine potatoes and onion in small bowl.

2. Lightly spray medium nonstick skillet with cooking spray. Add potato mixture; flatten with spatula. Cook 7 to 9 minutes per side or until both sides are lightly browned.

3. Mix tomato paste and water in small bowl; spread evenly over potatoes in skillet. Sprinkle with oregano.

4. Pour egg substitute over potato mixture. Cover; cook 4 minutes. Sprinkle mozzarella and bacon bits over egg. Cover; cook 1 minute.

5. Slide pizza from skillet onto serving plate. Cut into 4 wedges.　　*Makes 2 servings*

Nutrients per Serving: 2 wedges

Calories: 360, Calories from Fat: 22 %, Total Fat: 9 g, Saturated Fat: 4 g, Cholesterol: 15 mg, Sodium: 736 mg, Carbohydrate: 52 g, Fiber: 6 g, Protein: 21 g

Dietary Exchanges: 1 Vegetable, 3 Starch, 2 Meat

Individual Shepherd's Pie

Potato Mixture

    4 cups water
    1 large russet potato (about ½ pound), peeled and quartered
    ¼ cup hot fat-free (skim) milk
    2 teaspoons light butter
    ⅛ teaspoon salt
    Dash white pepper

Beef Mixture

    1 teaspoon olive oil
    2 tablespoons chopped onion
    1 clove garlic, minced
    1 cup chopped mushrooms
    ½ pound extra-lean ground beef
    1 tablespoon flour
    1 cup fat-free reduced-sodium beef broth
    2 small carrots, diced
    2 small parsnips, diced
    1 teaspoon dried parsley
    ⅛ teaspoon salt
    ⅛ teaspoon black pepper
    ½ cup frozen peas
    ¼ cup chopped leeks
    Paprika (optional)

1. Preheat oven to 400°F.

2. Bring water to a boil in medium saucepan over high heat. Boil potato until tender, about 15 to 18 minutes. Drain well. Mash potato with potato masher in medium bowl. Stir in hot milk, butter, salt and white pepper. Set aside.

3. Heat oil in large skillet over medium heat. Add onions and garlic; cook and stir until softened. Add mushrooms; cook and stir about 5 minutes or until mushrooms begin to brown. Spoon mixture into small bowl and set aside.

4. Brown beef 6 to 8 minutes in same skillet over medium-high heat, stirring to break up meat. Drain fat. Add mushroom mixture to beef. Sprinkle flour over beef mixture. Cook and stir 3 minutes over medium heat.

continued on page 58

Individual Shepherd's Pie, continued

5. Add broth, carrots, parsnips, parsley, salt and pepper. Bring to a boil. Reduce heat to a simmer; cook and stir until mixture thickens and carrots and parsnips are tender. Stir in peas and leeks. Spoon mixture into 2 (10-ounce) ovenproof ramekins.

6. Spoon mashed potatoes over meat mixture. Garnish with paprika. Place ramekins on baking sheet; bake 20 minutes or until heated through.   *Makes 2 servings*

Nutrients per Serving: ½ of total recipe

Calories: 473, Calories from Fat: 24 %, Total Fat: 13 g, Saturated Fat: 4 g, Cholesterol: 72 mg, Sodium: 486 mg, Carbohydrate: 57 g, Fiber: 10 g, Protein: 34 g

Dietary Exchanges: 3½ Starch, 4 Meat

Steak Diane with Cremini Mushrooms

      Nonstick cooking spray
  2 beef tenderloin steaks (4 ounces each), ¾ inch thick
  ¼ teaspoon black pepper
  ⅓ cup sliced shallots or chopped onion
  4 ounces cremini (brown or baby portobello) mushrooms, sliced
1½ tablespoons Worcestershire sauce
  1 tablespoon Dijon mustard

1. Lightly coat large nonstick skillet with cooking spray; heat over medium-high heat. Add steaks; sprinkle with pepper. Sear steaks 3 minutes per side for medium-rare (145°F) or longer to desired doneness. Transfer steaks to plate; set aside.

2. Lightly coat same skillet with cooking spray; heat over medium heat. Add shallots; cook and stir 2 minutes. Add mushrooms; cook and stir 3 minutes. Add Worcestershire sauce and mustard; cook and stir 1 minute.

3. Return steaks and any accumulated juices to skillet; heat through, turning once. Transfer steaks to 2 serving plates; top with mushroom mixture.   *Makes 2 servings*

Nutrients per Serving: ½ of total recipe

Calories: 239, Calories from Fat: 35 %, Total Fat: 9 g, Saturated Fat: 3 g, Cholesterol: 70 mg, Sodium: 302 mg, Carbohydrate: 10 g, Fiber: 1 g, Protein: 28 g

Dietary Exchanges: 1 Vegetable, 4 Meat

Autumn Pasta

1 boneless skinless chicken breast (about ¼ pound), cut into ½-inch cubes
8 brussels sprouts, trimmed and sliced
1 large bulb fennel, trimmed, quartered and sliced
2 medium tomatoes, seeded and chopped
¼ cup lemon juice
1 tablespoon olive oil
1 teaspoon minced garlic
   Nonstick cooking spray
1 cup cooked whole grain rotini pasta
2 tablespoons freshly grated Parmesan cheese

1. Combine chicken, brussels sprouts, fennel, tomatoes, lemon juice, oil and garlic in large bowl.

2. Lightly coat large skillet with cooking spray; heat over medium heat. Add chicken mixture; cook, covered, about 15 minutes or until vegetables are tender and chicken is cooked through, stirring occasionally.

3. Add pasta to skillet; cook until heated through. Sprinkle each serving with cheese.

Makes 2 servings

Nutrients per Serving: 2¼ cups pasta

Calories: 315, Calories from Fat: 26 %, Total Fat: 10 g, Saturated Fat: 2 g, Cholesterol: 37 mg, Sodium: 168 mg, Carbohydrate: 38 g, Fiber: 9 g, Protein: 23 g

Dietary Exchanges: 1 Vegetable, 2 Starch, 3 Meat

Salmon-Potato Cakes with Mustard Tartar Sauce

Salmon-Potato Cakes

    3 small unpeeled red potatoes (8 ounces), halved
    1 cup cooked flaked salmon
    1 egg white
    2 green onions, chopped
    1 tablespoon chopped fresh parsley
    ½ teaspoon Cajun or Creole seasoning mix
    1 teaspoon olive or canola oil

Mustard Tartar Sauce

    1 tablespoon reduced-fat mayonnaise
    1 tablespoon plain fat-free yogurt or fat-free sour cream
    1 tablespoon chopped fresh parsley
    1 tablespoon chopped dill pickle
    2 teaspoons coarse grain mustard
    1 teaspoon lemon juice

1. Place potatoes in small saucepan with about ½ cup water; bring to a boil. Reduce heat and simmer about 15 minutes or until potatoes are tender. Drain; mash potatoes with fork, leaving chunky texture.

2. Combine mashed potatoes, salmon, egg white, green onions, parsley and seasoning mix in medium bowl.

3. Heat oil in medium nonstick skillet over medium heat. Shape salmon mixture into 2 patties; place in skillet. Flatten slightly. Cook 7 minutes or until browned, turning halfway through cooking time.

4. Meanwhile, combine sauce ingredients in small bowl. Serve with cakes.

Makes 2 servings

Nutrients per Serving: 1 cake with 2 tablespoons sauce

Calories: 276, Calories from Fat: 37 %, Total Fat: 11 g, Saturated Fat: 2 g, Cholesterol: 52 mg, Sodium: 300 mg, Carbohydrate: 24 g, Fiber: 2 g, Protein: 19 g

Dietary Exchanges: 1½ Starch, 2 Meat, 1 Fat

Turkey Stroganoff

Nonstick cooking spray
2 cups sliced mushrooms
1 stalk celery, thinly sliced
1 medium shallot *or* ¼ small onion, minced
1 turkey tenderloin, turkey breast or boneless skinless chicken thighs (5 ounces), cut into bite-size chunks
½ cup reduced-sodium chicken broth
¼ teaspoon dried thyme
⅛ teaspoon black pepper
¼ cup fat-free sour cream
2 teaspoons all-purpose flour
⅛ teaspoon salt (optional)
⅔ cup cooked wide cholesterol-free whole wheat egg noodles

Slow Cooker Directions

1. Spray large skillet with cooking spray. Add mushrooms, celery and shallot. Cook and stir over medium heat 5 minutes or until mushrooms and shallot are tender. Spoon into small slow cooker. Add turkey, broth, thyme and pepper; stir. Cover; cook on LOW 5 to 6 hours.

2. Combine sour cream and flour in small bowl. Spoon 2 tablespoons liquid from slow cooker into bowl; stir well. Stir sour cream mixture into slow cooker. Cover; cook 10 minutes more. Stir in salt, if desired.

3. Spoon ⅓ cup cooked noodles onto each of 2 plates. Top with half of turkey mixture.

Makes 2 servings

Nutrients per Serving: 1 cup turkey mixture plus ⅓ cup noodles

Calories: 310, Calories from Fat: 9 %, Total Fat: 3 g, Saturated Fat: 1 g, Cholesterol: 100 mg, Sodium: 123 mg, Carbohydrate: 41 g, Fiber: 3 g, Protein: 30 g

Dietary Exchanges: 2 Starch, 3 Meat

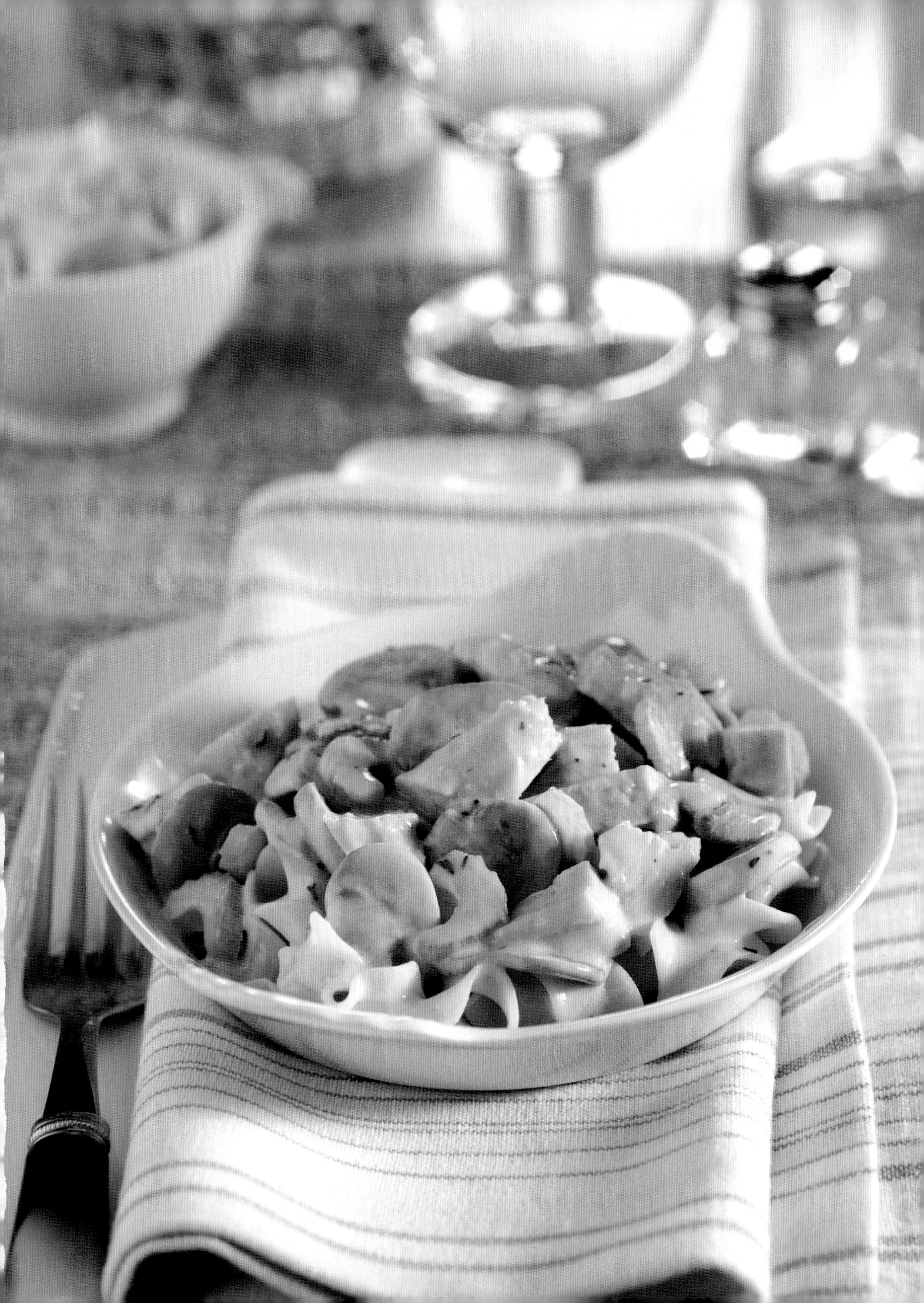

Rosemary-Garlic Scallops with Polenta

2 teaspoons olive oil

1 medium red bell pepper, sliced

⅓ cup chopped red onion

3 cloves garlic, minced

½ pound fresh bay scallops

2 teaspoons chopped fresh rosemary *or* ¾ teaspoon dried rosemary

¼ teaspoon black pepper

1¼ cups fat-free reduced-sodium chicken broth

½ cup cornmeal

¼ teaspoon salt

1. Heat oil in large nonstick skillet over medium heat. Add bell pepper, onion and garlic; cook and stir 5 minutes. Add scallops, rosemary and black pepper; cook and stir 3 to 5 minutes or until scallops are opaque.

2. Meanwhile, combine broth, cornmeal and salt in small saucepan. Bring to a boil over high heat. Reduce heat to low; simmer 5 minutes or until polenta is very thick, stirring frequently. Transfer to 2 serving plates. Top polenta with scallop mixture.

Makes 2 servings

Nutrients per Serving: 1¾ cups

Calories: 304, Calories from Fat: 23 %, Total Fat: 8 g, Saturated Fat: 1 g, Cholesterol: 53 mg, Sodium: 731 mg, Carbohydrate: 33 g, Fiber: 4 g, Protein: 26 g

Dietary Exchanges: 2 Starch, 3 Meat

Tip

If bay scallops are unavailable, large sea scallops cut into quarters would be the perfect substitute.

White Bean and Chicken Ragoût

2 boneless skinless chicken thighs
2 small carrots, cut into ½-inch pieces
2 medium celery stalks, cut into ½-inch pieces
¼ medium onion, chopped
1 bay leaf
1 sprig fresh parsley
1 clove garlic
1 sprig fresh thyme
3 black peppercorns
1 cup no-salt-added canned cannellini beans, rinsed and drained
1 plum tomato, chopped
1 teaspoon herbes de Provence
½ teaspoon salt
⅛ teaspoon black pepper
1 teaspoon extra-virgin olive oil
1 tablespoon chopped fresh parsley
Grated peel of 1 lemon

1. Place chicken in medium saucepan; add water to cover. Add carrots, celery, onion, bay leaf, parsley sprig, garlic, thyme and peppercorns. Bring to a boil; reduce heat to low. Simmer 15 to 20 minutes or until chicken is no longer pink in center and vegetables are tender.

2. Remove chicken from saucepan; let cool 5 minutes.

3. Drain vegetables; reserve 1 cup broth. Discard bay leaf, parsley, garlic, thyme and peppercorns.

4. When cool enough to handle, cut chicken into bite-size pieces. Return chicken to saucepan with vegetables. Stir in beans and tomato. Add herbes de Provence, salt and black pepper.

5. Stir reserved broth into mixture; simmer 5 minutes.

6. Divide between 2 bowls; drizzle with oil. Sprinkle with chopped parsley and lemon peel.

Makes 2 servings

Nutrients per Serving: 1½ cups ragoût

Calories: 283, Calories from Fat: 17 %, Total Fat: 6 g, Saturated Fat: <1 g, Cholesterol: 57 mg, Sodium: 715 mg, Carbohydrate: 36 g, Fiber: 10 g, Protein: 24 g

Dietary Exchanges: 2 Starch, 3 Meat

Side Dishes

Couscous Primavera

1 shallot, minced, *or* ¼ cup minced red onion
8 medium spears fresh asparagus, cooked and cut into 1-inch pieces
1 cup frozen peas
1 cup halved grape tomatoes
⅛ teaspoon salt
⅛ teaspoon black pepper
6 tablespoons whole wheat couscous
¼ cup grated Parmesan cheese

1. Coat large skillet with nonstick cooking spray. Add shallot; cook and stir over medium-high heat 3 minutes or until tender. Add asparagus and peas; cook and stir 2 minutes or until peas are heated through. Add tomatoes; cook and stir 2 minutes. Add salt, pepper and ½ cup water. Bring to a boil.

2. Stir in couscous. Cover; reduce heat to low. Simmer 3 minutes or until liquid is absorbed. Fluff with fork. Stir in Parmesan cheese. Serve immediately.

Makes 2 servings

Nutrients per Serving: 1⅓ cups

Calories: 303, Calories from Fat: 11 %, Total Fat: 4 g, Saturated Fat: 2 g, Cholesterol: 9 mg, Sodium: 363 mg, Carbohydrate: 53 g, Fiber: 12 g, Protein: 19 g

Dietary Exchanges: 2 Vegetable, 3 Starch, 1 Meat

Potato-Cabbage Pancakes

½ cup refrigerated fat-free shredded hash brown potatoes
½ cup lightly packed shredded coleslaw mix
¼ cup cholesterol-free egg substitute *or* 2 egg whites
¼ teaspoon white pepper
   Nonstick cooking spray
4 tablespoons unsweetened applesauce (optional)
2 tablespoons fat-free sour cream (optional)

1. Mix hash browns, coleslaw mix, egg substitute and pepper in medium bowl. Pack half of hash brown mixture into ½-cup measure.

2. Spray large nonstick skillet with cooking spray; place over medium-high heat.

3. Gently invert cup into skillet. Repeat with remaining hash brown mixture. Drizzle any juices from bowl over pancakes. When pancakes begin to sizzle, gently press with spatula to flatten to ½-inch thickness and 4 inches in diameter. Cook 4 to 5 minutes per side or until brown.

4. Top each pancake with 2 tablespoons applesauce or 1 tablespoon sour cream, if desired. *Makes 2 servings*

Hint: Double this recipe and place leftover Potato-Cabbage Pancakes in a freezer bag and freeze for later use.

Nutrients per Serving: 1 pancake

Calories: 82, Calories from Fat: 0 %, Total Fat: 0 g, Saturated Fat: 0 g, Cholesterol: 0 mg, Sodium: 74 mg, Carbohydrate: 17 g, Fiber: 2 g, Protein: 5 g

Dietary Exchanges: 1 Starch

Citrus Fruit Toss

2 tablespoons dried sweetened cranberries
2 tablespoons water
1 cup red grapefruit sections, drained
1 tablespoon sucralose-based sugar substitute
1 tablespoon fresh mint leaves, chopped
1½ teaspoons lime juice

1. Combine cranberries and water in microwavable bowl. Microwave on HIGH 1 minute; let stand 5 minutes. Drain well.

2. Combine cranberries, grapefruit, sugar substitute, mint and lime juice in medium bowl; toss gently. Let stand 5 minutes before serving.   *Makes 2 servings*

Nutrients per Serving: ½ cup fruit

Calories: 74, Calories from Fat: 2 %, Total Fat: <1 g, Saturated Fat: <1 g, Cholesterol: 0 mg, Sodium: <1 mg, Carbohydrate: 20 g, Fiber: 2 g, Protein: <1 g

Dietary Exchanges: 1 Fruit

Sweet Potato Fries

¼ teaspoon salt (kosher or sea salt preferred)
¼ teaspoon black pepper
¼ teaspoon ground red pepper
1 large sweet potato (about ½ pound)
2 teaspoons olive oil

1. Preheat oven to 350°F. Lightly coat baking sheet with nonstick cooking spray.

2. Mix together salt and peppers in small bowl.

3. Peel sweet potato; cut lengthwise into long spears. Toss with oil in medium bowl.

4. Place spears on baking sheet, leaving room between each spear. Sprinkle spears with salt mixture. Bake 45 minutes or until lightly browned.   *Makes 2 servings*

Nutrients per Serving: ½ of total recipe

Calories: 139, Calories from Fat: 29 %, Total Fat: 5 g, Saturated Fat: <1 g, Cholesterol: 0 mg, Sodium: 301 mg, Carbohydrate: 23 g, Fiber: 4 g, Protein: 2 g

Dietary Exchanges: 1½ Starch, 1 Fat

Barley Vegetable Casserole

⅓ cup uncooked barley (not quick-cooking)
1 cup plus 2 tablespoons vegetable broth, divided
2 cups frozen mixed vegetables (broccoli, cauliflower, carrots, onions)
¼ teaspoon garlic powder
¼ teaspoon black pepper
¼ teaspoon margarine
¼ teaspoon salt (optional)

1. Preheat oven to 350°F. Spray 1-quart casserole with nonstick cooking spray.

2. Place barley and 2 tablespoons broth in nonstick skillet; cook and stir over medium heat 3 minutes or until lightly browned. Transfer to prepared casserole.

3. Add vegetables, garlic powder, pepper and remaining 1 cup broth to casserole; mix well.

4. Cover and bake 50 minutes or until barley is tender and most of liquid is absorbed, stirring several times during baking. Stir in margarine and salt, if desired. Let stand 5 minutes before serving.

Makes 2 servings

Nutrients per Serving: ½ of total recipe

Calories: 155, Calories from Fat: 9 %, Total Fat: 1 g, Saturated Fat: 0 g, Cholesterol: 0 mg, Sodium: 298 mg, Carbohydrate: 30 g, Fiber: 8 g, Protein: 5 g

Dietary Exchanges: 3 Vegetable, 1 Starch

Lime-Ginger Coleslaw

1 cup shredded green cabbage
¾ cup matchstick-size carrots
½ cup shredded red cabbage
2 tablespoons finely chopped green onion
1½ tablespoons lime juice
1 tablespoon sugar substitute
1 tablespoon chopped fresh cilantro
1 teaspoon vegetable or canola oil
¾ teaspoon grated fresh ginger
   Dash salt
   Dash red pepper flakes (optional)

Combine all ingredients in large bowl. Toss well. Let stand 10 minutes before serving.

Makes 2 servings

Nutrients per Serving: 1 cup coleslaw

Calories: 58, Calories from Fat: 7 %, Total Fat: 2 g, Saturated Fat: 1 g, Cholesterol: 0 mg, Sodium: 106 mg, Carbohydrate: 10 g, Fiber: 2 g, Protein: 2 g

Dietary Exchanges: 2 Vegetable

Tip

Don't save coleslaw just for grilling season. It makes a healthy and delicious side dish any time of the year.

Sweet Endings

Pumpkin Bread Pudding

2 slices whole wheat bread
1 cup pumpkin purée
3 tablespoons egg substitute
2 tablespoons sucralose-based sugar substitute
1 tablespoon raisins
1 teaspoon vanilla
½ teaspoon ground cinnamon
    Fat-free whipped topping (optional)

1. Preheat oven to 375°F. Lightly spray 2 ovenproof ramekins with nonstick cooking spray.

2. Toast bread; cut into 1-inch cubes and set aside.

3. Whisk pumpkin, egg substitute, sugar substitute, raisins, vanilla and cinnamon in medium bowl until blended. Fold in toast cubes.

4. Spoon batter evenly into ramekins; bake 30 minutes. Serve warm with whipped topping, if desired. *Makes 2 servings*

Nutrients per Serving: ½ of total recipe

Calories: 141, Calories from Fat: 8 %, Total Fat: 1 g, Saturated Fat: <1 g, Cholesterol: 0 mg, Sodium: 177 mg, Carbohydrate: 28 g, Fiber: 5 g, Protein: 6 g

Dietary Exchanges: 2 Starch

Individual Tiramisù Cups

4 whole ladyfingers, broken into bite-size pieces
6 tablespoons cold strong coffee
2 packets sugar substitute
½ teaspoon vanilla
½ cup fat-free whipped topping
1½ teaspoons unsweetened cocoa powder
1 tablespoon sliced almonds

1. Divide ladyfinger pieces between 2 small dessert bowls.

2. Combine coffee, sugar substitute and vanilla in small bowl; stir until sugar substitute is dissolved. Spoon evenly over each serving of ladyfinger pieces.

3. Place whipped topping in small bowl. Fold in cocoa until blended. Spoon evenly over ladyfingers. Cover with plastic wrap and refrigerate at least 2 hours.

4. Meanwhile, heat almonds in small skillet over medium high heat; toast 2 to 3 minutes or until golden, stirring constantly. Remove from heat; cool completely.

5. Sprinkle almonds over desserts just before serving.   *Makes 2 servings*

Nutrients per Serving: ½ cup

Calories: 148, Calories from Fat: 28 %, Total Fat: 5 g, Saturated Fat: 1 g, Cholesterol: 80 mg, Sodium: 43 mg, Carbohydrate: 22 g, Fiber: 1 g, Protein: 4 g

Dietary Exchanges: 1½ Starch, 1 Fat

"Moo-vin" Strawberry Milk Shake

1 pint low-fat sugar-free vanilla ice cream
1 cup thawed frozen unsweetened strawberries
¼ cup fat-free (skim) milk
¼ teaspoon vanilla

Combine all ingredients in blender; blend until smooth. Pour into 2 small glasses. Serve immediately.   *Makes 2 servings*

Nutrients per Serving: 1 milk shake

Calories: 217, Calories from Fat: 26 %, Total Fat: 7 g, Saturated Fat: 3 g, Cholesterol: 21 mg, Sodium: 118 mg, Carbohydrate: 34 g, Fiber: 1 g, Protein: 8 g

Dietary Exchanges: 2½ Starch, 1 Fat

Baked Pear Dessert

⅓ cup unsweetened apple cider or apple juice, divided
2 tablespoons dried cranberries or raisins
1 tablespoon toasted sliced almonds
⅛ teaspoon ground cinnamon
1 medium unpeeled pear (about 6 ounces), cut in half lengthwise and cored
½ cup low-fat sugar-free vanilla ice cream or frozen yogurt

1. Preheat oven to 350°F. Combine 1 teaspoon cider, cranberries, almonds and cinnamon in small bowl.

2. Place pear halves, cut sides up, in small baking dish. Evenly mound almond mixture on top of pear halves. Pour remaining cider into dish; cover with foil.

3. Bake 35 to 40 minutes or until pears are soft, spooning cider in dish over pears once or twice during baking. Serve warm with ice cream. *Makes 2 servings*

Nutrients per Serving: 1 pear half with ¼ cup ice cream

Calories: 87, Calories from Fat: 19 %, Total Fat: 2 g, Saturated Fat: <1 g, Cholesterol: 3 mg, Sodium: 13 mg, Carbohydrate: 16 g, Fiber: 1 g, Protein: 1 g

Dietary Exchanges: 1 Fruit, ½ Fat

"Moo-vin" Chocolate Milk Shake

1 pint low-fat sugar-free chocolate ice cream
½ cup fat-free (skim) milk
1 tablespoon chocolate syrup
¼ teaspoon vanilla

Combine all ingredients in blender; blend until smooth. Pour into 2 small glasses. Serve immediately. *Makes 2 servings*

Nutrients per Serving: 1 milk shake

Calories: 249, Calories from Fat: 18 %, Total Fat: 5 g, Saturated Fat: 3 g, Cholesterol: 12 mg, Sodium: 179 mg, Carbohydrate: 43 g, Fiber: <1 g, Protein: 10 g

Dietary Exchanges: 3 Starch, 1 Fat

Sweet 'n Easy Fruit Crisp Bowls

2 tablespoons low-fat granola with almonds
Nonstick cooking spray
1 red apple such as Gala (8 ounces), diced into ½-inch pieces
1 tablespoon dried sweetened cranberries
¼ teaspoon apple pie spice or ground cinnamon
1 teaspoon diet margarine
1 packet sugar substitute
¼ teaspoon almond extract
2 tablespoons low-fat vanilla ice cream

1. Place granola in small resealable food storage bag; crush lightly to form coarse crumbs. Set aside. Coat large skillet with cooking spray; heat over medium heat. Add apple, cranberries and apple pie spice; cook and stir 4 minutes or until apple is just tender.

2. Remove from heat; stir in margarine, sugar substitute and almond extract. Spoon into 2 dessert bowls or dessert plates. Sprinkle with granola and spoon ice cream on top. Serve immediately.   *Makes 2 servings*

Note: You may make apple mixture up to 8 hours in advance and top with granola and ice cream at time of serving. To rewarm crisp, microwave apple mixture (before adding granola and ice cream) 20 to 30 seconds on HIGH or until slightly heated.

Nutrients per Serving: ½ of total recipe

Calories: 150, Calories from Fat: 15 %, Total Fat: 3 g, Saturated Fat: <1 g, Cholesterol: <1 mg, Sodium: 40 mg, Carbohydrate: 32 g, Fiber: 4 g, Protein: 1 g

Dietary Exchanges: 2 Fruit, ½ Fat

Individual Pear Upside-Down Cakes

2 tablespoons no-sugar-added strawberry fruit spread

1 pear, halved, cored and very thinly sliced

¼ cup cake flour

1 tablespoon plus 1½ teaspoons sucralose-based sugar substitute, divided

3 egg whites

¼ teaspoon cream of tartar

½ teaspoon vanilla

Microwave Directions

1. Lightly spray 2 large microwavable coffee cups with nonstick cooking spray. Place 1 tablespoon strawberry fruit spread in each cup. Layer pear slices over fruit spread. Set aside.

2. Sift together flour and 1 tablespoon sugar substitute in medium bowl; set aside.

3. Beat egg whites in large bowl with electric mixer at high speed until foamy. Add cream of tartar; beat until almost stiff. Gradually add remaining 1½ teaspoons sugar substitute; beat at high speed 1 minute. Fold in vanilla, then flour mixture. Pour batter into prepared coffee cups. Microwave on HIGH 3 minutes.

4. Turn cakes out onto dessert plates. Serve hot or cold.   *Makes 2 servings*

Nutrients per Serving: 1 cake

Calories: 138, Calories from Fat: 2 %, Total Fat: <1 g, Saturated Fat: <1 g, Cholesterol: 0 mg, Sodium: 85 mg, Carbohydrate: 30 g, Fiber: 3 g, Protein: 7 g

Dietary Exchanges: 1 Fruit, 2 Starch

Fudge, Apple and Pecan Tizzies

2 tablespoons sucralose-based sugar substitute
½ teaspoon ground cinnamon
½ teaspoon cocoa powder
1 apple, cored and cut into 8 wedges
2 tablespoons sugar-free fat-free hot fudge topping
8 pecan halves, broken in half again

1. Mix sugar substitute, cinnamon and cocoa powder together in small bowl.

2. Place apple wedges on plate; sprinkle with cocoa mixture. Turn apple slices over and sprinkle other side.

3. Spread each apple wedge evenly with hot fudge topping. Top with 2 pecan halves. Refrigerate at least 20 minutes before serving.   *Makes 2 servings*

Nutrients per Serving: 4 pieces

Calories: 143, Calories from Fat: 34 %, Total Fat: 6 g, Saturated Fat: <1 g, Cholesterol: 0 mg, Sodium: 19 mg, Carbohydrate: 24 g, Fiber: 3 g, Protein: 1 g

Dietary Exchanges: 1½ Starch, 1 Fat

"Moo-vin" Vanilla Milk Shake

1 pint low-fat sugar-free vanilla ice cream
½ cup fat-free (skim) milk
½ teaspoon vanilla

Combine all ingredients in blender; blend until smooth. Pour into 2 small glasses. Serve immediately.   *Makes 2 servings*

Nutrients per Serving: 1 milk shake

Calories: 204, Calories from Fat: 27 %, Total Fat: 6 g, Saturated Fat: 3 g, Cholesterol: 21 mg, Sodium: 132 mg, Carbohydrate: 29 g, Fiber: 0 g, Protein: 8 g

Dietary Exchanges: 2 Starch, 1 Fat

VOLUME MEASUREMENTS (dry)

$1/8$ teaspoon = 0.5 mL
$1/4$ teaspoon = 1 mL
$1/2$ teaspoon = 2 mL
$3/4$ teaspoon = 4 mL
1 teaspoon = 5 mL
1 tablespoon = 15 mL
2 tablespoons = 30 mL
$1/4$ cup = 60 mL
$1/3$ cup = 75 mL
$1/2$ cup = 125 mL
$2/3$ cup = 150 mL
$3/4$ cup = 175 mL
1 cup = 250 mL
2 cups = 1 pint = 500 mL
3 cups = 750 mL
4 cups = 1 quart = 1 L

VOLUME MEASUREMENTS (fluid)

1 fluid ounce (2 tablespoons) = 30 mL
4 fluid ounces ($1/2$ cup) = 125 mL
8 fluid ounces (1 cup) = 250 mL
12 fluid ounces ($1\frac{1}{2}$ cups) = 375 mL
16 fluid ounces (2 cups) = 500 mL

WEIGHTS (mass)

$1/2$ ounce = 15 g
1 ounce = 30 g
3 ounces = 90 g
4 ounces = 120 g
8 ounces = 225 g
10 ounces = 285 g
12 ounces = 360 g
16 ounces = 1 pound = 450 g

DIMENSIONS

$1/16$ inch = 2 mm
$1/8$ inch = 3 mm
$1/4$ inch = 6 mm
$1/2$ inch = 1.5 cm
$3/4$ inch = 2 cm
1 inch = 2.5 cm

OVEN TEMPERATURES

250°F = 120°C
275°F = 140°C
300°F = 150°C
325°F = 160°C
350°F = 180°C
375°F = 190°C
400°F = 200°C
425°F = 220°C
450°F = 230°C

BAKING PAN SIZES

Utensil	Size in Inches/Quarts	Metric Volume	Size in Centimeters
Baking or Cake Pan (square or rectangular)	$8 \times 8 \times 2$	2 L	$20 \times 20 \times 5$
	$9 \times 9 \times 2$	2.5 L	$23 \times 23 \times 5$
	$12 \times 8 \times 2$	3 L	$30 \times 20 \times 5$
	$13 \times 9 \times 2$	3.5 L	$33 \times 23 \times 5$
Loaf Pan	$8 \times 4 \times 3$	1.5 L	$20 \times 10 \times 7$
	$9 \times 5 \times 3$	2 L	$23 \times 13 \times 7$
Round Layer Cake Pan	$8 \times 1\frac{1}{2}$	1.2 L	20×4
	$9 \times 1\frac{1}{2}$	1.5 L	23×4
Pie Plate	$8 \times 1\frac{1}{4}$	750 mL	20×3
	$9 \times 1\frac{1}{4}$	1 L	23×3
Baking Dish or Casserole	1 quart	1 L	—
	$1\frac{1}{2}$ quart	1.5 L	—
	2 quart	2 L	—